Y0-BYZ-145

A WORLD OF RECIPES

India

REVISED AND UPDATED

Julie McCulloch

Heinemann Library
Chicago, Illinois

www.heinemannraintree.com
Visit our website to find out
more information about
Heinemann-Raintree books.

To order:

☎ Phone 888-454-2279

💻 Visit www.heinemannraintree.com
to browse our catalog and order online.

Edited by David Andrews and Diyan Leake
Designed by Richard Parker
Illustrated by Nicholas Beresford-Davis
Picture research by Mica Brancic
Printed and bound in China by Leo Paper Products Ltd

13 12 11 10 09
10 9 8 7 6 5 4 3 2 1

New edition ISBN: 978-1-4329-2234-4

**The Library of Congress has cataloged the first edition
as follows:**
McCulloch, Julie, 1973-.
   India/Julie McCulloch.
     p. cm. -- (A world of recipes)
   Includes bibliographical references and index.
   ISBN 978-1-58810-085-6 (HC) ISBN 978-1-58810-387-1
(PB)
             Cookery, India—Juvenile literature. [1. Cookery,
India. 2.India –Social life and customs.] I. McCulloch, Julie,
1973- World of recipes
TX724.5.I4 M39 2001
641.5954—dc22   00-063273

Acknowledgments

The author and publishers are grateful to the following for
permission to reproduce copyright material: © Capstone
Global Library Ltd/MM Studios pp. 40, 41; Gareth Boden pp.
8–39, 42, 43; Photolibrary Group pp. 5 (Iconotec/Alamer), 6
(age fotostock/Dinodia Dinodia), 7 (Oxford Scientific (OSF)/
Mike Powles).

Cover photograph of a balti chicken curry with naan and
spices reproduced with permission of Photolibrary Group
(Fresh Food Images/Martin Brigdale).

Every effort has been made to contact copyright holders of
any material reproduced in this book. Any omissions will
be rectified in subsequent printings if notice is given to the
publisher.

All the Internet addresses (URLs) given in this book were valid
at the time of going to press. However, due to the dynamic
nature of the Internet, some addresses may have changed, or
sites may have changed or ceased to exist since publication.
While the author and Publishers regret any inconvenience this
may cause readers, no responsibility for any such changes can
be accepted by either the author or the Publishers.

Contents

Some words are shown in bold, **like this**. You can find out what they mean by looking in the glossary.

India

feet HEIGHT meters	
over 13,120	over 4,000
6,560–13,120	2,000–4,000
3,277–6,557	1,000–1,999
1,640–3,277	500–999
656–1,637	200–499
under 656	under 200

Typhoons, tea, and tigers can all be found on the huge peninsula of India. This **tropical** country has the second largest population on Earth.

Reaching southward from Asia, India is surrounded by ocean on two sides. The world's highest mountains—the Himalayas—are in northern India. Below them, in the valleys of the Indus and Ganges rivers, **fertile** plains are home to millions of people. India also contains a northern desert, and hilly plains in the center and south.

This diverse geography affects the climate. The Himalaya Mountains are cold enough to contain glaciers. The rest of India is hot and dry. **Monsoon** winds bring rain to the coasts in summer. Typhoons, or hurricanes, sweep in from the sea and cause flooding.

In the past

India was home to one of the world's oldest civilizations. The Indus people built cities in the Indus River valley about 5,000 years ago. Around 1500 BCE, Aryan invaders from the north introduced the Sanskrit language and the early Hindu religion.

The Aryans also brought a **caste** system. It divided people into five groups: priests and leaders, warriors, farmers and traders, servants, and untouchables. Each person was born into a caste. People from different castes did not eat together, make friends, or marry one another. People remained in the same caste for life.

India was later invaded by the Persians and the Mongols. The British took control of India for about 100 years and began exporting tea, spices, and cotton from there. India became independent in 1947, after a peaceful man, Mohandas Gandhi, led people in non-violent protests. Indians gave him the name Mahatma, which means "great soul."

India today

The ancient Aryan culture and religion are still present. Today, 80 percent of Indians are Hindus who believe in being peaceful and non-violent. Hindus do not kill, and many eat only a **vegetarian** diet with no meat. Hindus believe that cows are **sacred** animals, and so eating beef is strictly forbidden. The caste system continues to influence people's roles in society.

↑ Cows mingle safely in the busy traffic of India's cities.

Indian Food

Spicy and hot, cool and soothing, sour and sweet—Indian cooking is about balancing contrasts!

Around the country

Since Aryan times, rice and wheat have been grown beside the Indus and Ganges rivers. Their valleys contain the world's largest area of fertile mud. The flat land makes it easy to build canals to take water to the crops. There are few trees to get in the way.

In areas such as Gujarat, where many Hindu people live, hardly any meat is eaten. In areas where Muslim people live, no pork is eaten, since the Islamic religion forbids this. In other areas, such as the Punjab, chicken is especially popular. It is cooked in the tandoori style, using a large clay oven with a coal fire. Tandoori chicken has a spicy, smoky taste.

↑ Rice grows in the fertile plains along the rivers of India.

Many other dishes are spicy, especially in Bengal, where cooks use aniseed, cumin, mustard, and fenugreek. Hot food is balanced with cool food such as yogurt or coconut milk. Traditional Indian doctors believe in creating balance in the body through food.

Indian meals

Lunch is the most important meal. Many people travel home from work to eat lunch. Other people have traditional hot food delivered to work by a catering service. The evening meal is usually lighter than lunch.

Indians use their right hand to eat. Hands are washed before and after every meal. Naan and chapatis (wheat flat breads) are also used to scoop up food. Sticky rice balls are used instead of spoons for dipping into soup.

Meals often consist of several small dishes, all served at the same time. Salads and very sweet desserts are often prepared. Eating from a metal plate or a banana leaf is common.

Tea, please!

India is famous for growing tea bushes, especially around Darjeeling. Chai is tea prepared with milk, sugar, and spices (ginger, cloves, and cardamom). This is drunk with breakfast and in the late afternoon. A popular cold drink is lassi, which is buttermilk or yogurt flavored with rose petals or mangoes.

↑ This woman is picking tea in the Assam region of India.

Ingredients

chapati

naan

ghee

red
lentils

coconut
milk

rice

turmeric

creamed
coconut

cumin

garam
masala

ground
coriander

chili powder

Bread

Bread is often served as an accompaniment in India, and there are many
different types. Chapatis are thin and round, and cooked in a hot pan
(see page 32). Naan bread is thick and soft, and cooked in an oven.
Supermarkets often sell ready-made chapatis and naans.

Coconut

Coconut is used in many dishes, especially in southern India. You may find
fresh coconuts in stores, but it is easier to buy it pre-processed. The recipes
in this book use coconut in two forms—coconut milk, which comes in cans,
and dried coconut, which is shredded and sold in packages. Indian cooking
also uses blocks of creamed coconut. However, these are often difficult to
find in supermarkets, so they are not included in these recipes.

Garlic

Garlic is used in many dishes, especially those from northern India. You can buy garlic in the vegetable section of most supermarkets.

Ginger

Fresh ginger is used in many Indian dishes, usually **peeled** and **grated** or finely **chopped**. It is readily available in supermarkets. It is better to use fresh rather than dried ginger, because the taste is stronger.

Lentils

Lentils are an important part of many people's diets in India, especially **vegetarians**. They are cheap and good for you. There are many different types of lentil. The most common type, red lentils, can be found in most supermarkets.

Oil

Most savory Indian dishes are cooked in ghee. Ghee is a type of purified butter. It gives a rich, buttery taste to Indian food. Ghee can be difficult to find, so the recipes in this book use vegetable oil or corn oil.

Rice

Rice is an important ingredient in Indian cooking. It comes in two main types: short grain and long grain. Long-grain rice (especially an Indian rice called basmati) is more suitable for most Indian dishes.

Spices

Spices are plants or seeds with strong flavors, which are used to add taste. They are an essential ingredient in many Indian dishes. Some of the most common spices are cumin, turmeric, coriander, garam masala, and chili powder (see page 13 for more about coriander and page 27 for garam masala). You only need to use small amounts of spices. Chili powder is very hot, so you may prefer to use less, or leave it out if you do not like food that is too spicy. All of these spices can easily be bought dried in jars or boxes.

Before You Start

Which recipe should I try?

The recipes you choose to make depend on many things. Some recipes make a good main course, while others are better as starters. Some are easy, while others are more difficult.

The top right-hand page of each recipe has information that can help you. It tells you how long each recipe will take and how many people it serves. You can multiply or divide the quantities if you want to cook for more or fewer people. This section also shows how difficult each dish is to make: the recipes are easy (*), medium (**), or difficult (***) to cook. The symbols in the corner can help you quickly find certain recipes. Here is a key that will help you.

Healthy choice: These recipes are healthy to eat.

Quick and easy: These recipes are quick and easy to make.

Sweet treat: These recipes make a good dessert or sweet snack.

This symbol ⚠ is a sign of a dangerous step in a recipe. For these steps, be extra careful or ask an adult to help.

Kitchen rules

There are a few basic rules you should always follow when you cook:

- Ask an adult if you can use the kitchen.
- Wash your hands before you start.
- Wear an apron to protect your clothes. Tie back long hair.
- Be very careful when using sharp knives.
- Never leave pan handles sticking out—it could be dangerous if you bump into them.
- Always wear oven mits to lift things in and out of the oven.
- Wash fruits and vegetables before you use them.

Quantities and measurements

Ingredients for recipes can be measured in two different ways. Imperial measurements use cups, pounds, ounces, and fluid ounces. Metric measurements use grams, liters, and milliliters. In the recipes in this book you will see the following abbreviations:

tbsp = tablespoons   oz. = ounces   cm = centimeters
tsp = teaspoons   g = grams   ml = milliliters
lbs = pounds   in. = inchesli

Utensils

To cook the recipes in this book, you will need these utensils, as well as kitchen essentials, such as spoons, plates, and bowls.

- Chopping board
- **Colander** or sieve
- Dish towel
- Food processor or blender
- Frying pan
- Grater
- Kitchen scale
- Measuring cup (for liquids)
- Measuring cups (for dry ingredients) and measuring spoons
- Rolling pin
- Saucepan with lid
- Sharp knife
- Spatula

Lima Beans with Raisins

Beans are used in many Indian dishes and are a very good source of **protein**. This simple bean dish could be served as a starter or as an accompaniment to a main course.

What you need

1 tbsp fresh cilantro leaves (see page 13)

1 tbsp oil

1½ cups canned lima beans

¼ tsp turmeric

¼ tsp chili powder (optional)

2 tbsp golden raisins

1 tsp sugar

1 tbsp lemon juice

What you do

1 Finely **chop** the cilantro.

2 **Drain** the liquid from the lima beans by emptying them into a sieve or **colander**.

3 Heat the oil in a frying pan over medium heat.

4 Add the lima beans and cook for one minute.

5 Turn the heat down to low. Add the turmeric, chili powder (if using), raisins, sugar, and lemon juice. Cook for another five minutes.

6 Add 2 tbsp of water and **simmer** for five minutes.

7 **Sprinkle** the chopped cilantro over the beans and raisins before serving.

CILANTRO AND CORIANDER

Coriander is used in two forms in Indian food: fresh coriander leaves (an herb known as cilantro) and ground coriander (a spice). Cilantro has a strong, fresh taste. It is used for its flavor, to add decoration, and for the bright green color it gives to sauces. You need about as many leaves as will fit in a tablespoon for the recipes in this book. Ground coriander is made from the crushed seeds of the coriander plant. Ground coriander is added to many Indian dishes and adds a strong, slightly lemony taste.

Fish and Coconut Soup

Savory Indian dishes are not traditionally divided into starters or main courses. Several small dishes are usually all served at the same time. This soup would be just one of them.

What you need

½ onion

1 clove garlic

A small piece of fresh ginger (about 1 in. long)

2 skinless cod fillets

1 tbsp oil

1 tsp turmeric

¼ tsp chili powder (optional)

2 cups reduced-fat coconut milk

1 tbsp lemon juice

This recipe suggests using cod, but you could use any sort of white fish. Try to find fish fillets without the skin on. If you use frozen fish, take it out of the freezer and put it into the refrigerator at least 12 hours before using it, so that it is completely **thawed**.

What you do

1 **Peel** the skin from the onion and finely **chop** it.

2 Peel the skin from the garlic clove and ginger and finely chop them.

3 Cut the cod fillets into small pieces.

4 Heat the oil in a saucepan over medium heat. Add the chopped onion, garlic, ginger, turmeric, and chili powder (if using), and **fry** for five minutes.

5 Add the coconut milk and bring the mixture to a **boil**.

6 Add the fish pieces and lemon juice. Turn the heat down to medium and **simmer** the soup for 10 minutes.

Spicy Scrambled Eggs

The Parsi people, who live in western India, originally came from the land that is now Iran. When they arrived in India, they brought with them many egg dishes, like this recipe for scrambled eggs. In India, this dish may be eaten for breakfast, with tea in the middle of the day, or for dinner.

What you need

A small piece of fresh ginger (about 1 in. long)

1 clove of garlic

½ onion

1 tbsp fresh cilantro leaves (see page 13)

3 eggs

1 tbsp oil

¼ tsp chili powder (optional)

¼ tsp turmeric

What you do

1 **Peel** the skin from the ginger and garlic and finely **chop** them.

2 Peel the skin from the onion and finely chop it.

3 Finely chop the cilantro leaves.

4 Crack the eggs into a small bowl. **Beat** them with a fork or a whisk until the yolk and the white are mixed.

5 Heat the oil in a saucepan over medium heat. Add the chopped ginger, garlic, onion, chili powder (if using), and turmeric, and **fry** for five minutes.

6 Add the beaten eggs and chopped cilantro. Cook for five minutes, stirring often with a wooden spoon, until the eggs start to become solid. Serve immediately.

Shrimp Patia

Patia is a sweet and sour dish—the honey gives the sweet taste, and the vinegar the sourness. Serve with plain boiled rice (see recipe on page 19) or with the pilau rice recipe (see page 30).

What you need

½ onion

1 clove garlic

A small piece of fresh ginger (about 1 in. long)

1 tbsp oil

½ tsp cumin

½ tsp turmeric

½ tsp ground coriander

1 tsp paprika

2 tbsp plain yogurt

1 tbsp honey

2 tsp vinegar

11 oz. cooked peeled shrimp

1 tbsp fresh cilantro leaves (see page 13)

What you do

 Peel the skin from the onion and finely **chop** it.

 Peel the garlic and ginger and finely chop them.

3 Heat the oil in a saucepan over medium heat. Add the chopped onion, garlic, ginger, cumin, turmeric, ground coriander, and paprika, and **fry** for five minutes.

 Reduce the heat, add the yogurt, honey, and vinegar, and **simmer** for five minutes.

5 Add the shrimp and simmer the mixture for another five minutes.

6 Finely chop the fresh cilantro leaves and **sprinkle** them over your patia.

PLAIN BOILED RICE

This recipe makes enough plain boiled rice for two people:

1 Put 1 cup (140 g) of rice into a saucepan.

2 Add 2 cups (400 ml) of water.

3 Bring to a **boil**, then simmer for 20 minutes, stirring occasionally, until the rice has soaked up all the water.

Banana Curry

This fruity curry (see page 21) has a sweet, spicy taste. It is best to use unripe bananas, which are still slightly green, to make this dish.

What you need

A small piece of fresh
  ginger (about
  1 in. long)
2 bananas
1 tbsp oil
½ tsp garam masala
  (see page 27)
½ tsp cumin
¼ tsp chili powder
  (optional)
½ tsp turmeric
1 cup plain yogurt
1 tbsp lemon juice

What you do

1 **Peel** the skin from the ginger and finely **chop** it.

2 Peel the bananas and cut them into slices about ½ in. (1 cm) thick.

⚠ 3 Heat the oil in a saucepan over medium heat. Add the chopped ginger, garam masala, cumin, chili powder (if using), and turmeric, and **fry** for about three minutes.

4 Add the pieces of banana and stir them into the spices until they are well coated.

5 Reduce the heat and add the yogurt and lemon juice. **Simmer** the curry for 10 minutes.

WHAT IS A CURRY?

The word *curry* is used to describe any spicy
Indian dish. Indian people don't use the word,
and no one knows for sure where it came from.
One theory is that *curry* may have come from the
Indian word *karahi*, which is a type of frying pan
used all over India for cooking spices.

Spicy Chickpeas

This is a very filling **vegetarian** dish. Like beans and lentils, chickpeas are an important source of **protein**. You could eat this dish the Indian way, by tearing off pieces of chapati (see page 32) and using them to scoop up the chickpeas.

What you need

- 1 clove of garlic
- 1 onion
- 2 tomatoes
- ½ cup canned chickpeas
- ¼ tsp chili powder (optional)
- 1 tbsp oil
- ¼ tsp ground coriander (see page 13)
- ½ tsp garam masala (see page 27)
- ½ tsp turmeric
- 1 tbsp lemon juice

What you do

1 **Peel** the skin from the garlic and onion and finely **chop** them.

2 Chop the tomatoes into small pieces.

3 **Drain** the liquid from the chickpeas by emptying the can into a **colander** or sieve.

4 Heat the oil in a saucepan over medium heat. Add the chopped garlic, onion, chili powder (if using), coriander, garam masala, and turmeric, and **fry** for five minutes.

5 Add the chopped tomatoes, chickpeas, and lemon juice. Cook for 10 minutes.

LUCKY CHICKPEAS

Chickpeas are known as *channa* in India. Many Hindus eat *channa* on Fridays, because they believe this will bring them luck.

Vegetable Biryani

A "biryani" is a dish made of rice with other ingredients added to it. It makes a filling main course.

What you need

½ onion
1 clove garlic
½ carrot
1 zucchini
1 vegetable stock cube
1 tbsp oil
1 tsp ground cinnamon
½ tsp turmeric
½ tsp garam masala
    (see page 27)
½ cup rice
½ cup fresh or frozen
    peas
½ cup chopped
    mixed nuts
¼ cup raisins

What you do

1 **Peel** the skin from the onion and garlic and finely **chop** them.

2 Wash the carrot, then cut it into small pieces.

3 Cut off the top and bottom of the zucchini, then **slice** one half of it. Cut each slice into four.

4 Put 2 cups (450 ml) of water into a saucepan and bring it to a **boil**. Crumble the stock cube into the water and stir until it **dissolves**. Put the stock to one side.

5 Heat the oil in a saucepan over medium heat. Add the chopped onion, garlic, cinnamon, turmeric, and garam masala, and **fry** for about three minutes.

6 Add the rice and fry for another five minutes, stirring occasionally.

7 Add the chopped carrot, zucchini, peas, and vegetable stock. Stir well, then reduce the heat to low and **cover** the pan.

8 **Simmer** the mixture for about 20 minutes, stirring from time to time, until all the liquid has been soaked up and the rice is soft.

9 Stir in the chopped nuts and raisins, then serve.

MORE BIRYANIS
There are many different variations on the basic biryani. You could make a meat biryani by adding some chopped-up cooked chicken, or a seafood biryani by adding cooked shrimp or fish.

Spicy Okra

Okra is a vegetable that grows in many parts of India. It is also known as *bindi* or ladies' fingers. Okra does not have a very strong flavor, but is excellent at picking up the taste of spices in a dish. When you cook okra, you will see that it produces lots of sticky "threads." This is perfectly normal! If you cannot find okra, try making this dish with eggplant instead. **Chop** an eggplant into ½-in. (1-cm) cubes, then cook it in the same way as the okra.

What You need

1 onion

2 cloves garlic

2 tomatoes

2½ cups okra

1 tbsp oil

1 tsp ground coriander
(see page 13)

½ tsp turmeric

1 tsp garam masala
(see page 27)

What You do

1 **Peel** the skin from the onion and garlic and finely chop them.

2 Chop the tomatoes into pieces.

3 Cut the tops and bottoms off the okra, then cut the okra into ½-in. (1-cm) slices.

4 Heat the oil in a saucepan over medium heat. Add the chopped onion, garlic, coriander, turmeric, and garam masala, and **fry** for five minutes.

5 Reduce the heat and add the okra slices and chopped tomatoes. **Simmer** the mixture for 10 minutes.

GARAM MASALA

Garam masala means "hot mixture." It is a mixture of spices that is added to many Indian dishes to add flavor. You can buy ready-mixed garam masala in jars or boxes, but most Indian cooks make their own. It is made by **toasting** black peppercorns, cinnamon, cloves, coriander, and cumin in a frying pan without oil, then **grinding** the toasted spices into a fine powder.

27

Lentil Patties

Over 60 varieties of lentils are grown in India. The most common are red lentils, although other types of lentils could also be used in this dish. Check on the package to see if they need soaking first.

What You need

- 2 green onions
- 1 tbsp fresh cilantro leaves (see page 13)
- ½ cup lentils
- 1 cup water
- ¼ tsp chili powder (optional)
- ½ tsp turmeric
- 3 tbsp all-purpose flour
- 2 tbsp oil

What You do

1 Cut the tops and bottoms off the green onions and finely **chop** them.

2 Finely chop the cilantro leaves.

3 Put the lentils into a saucepan with the water. Bring the water to a **boil**, then reduce the heat. **Cover** the pan and **simmer** the lentils for about 20 minutes, until the lentils have soaked up all the water.

4 Add the chopped green onions, cilantro, chili powder (if using), turmeric, and flour. Mix everything together well.

5 Rub a bit of oil into your hands so that the mixture does not stick, then divide the lentil mixture into six pieces. Form each piece into a ball. Flatten each ball into a patty.

Heat the rest of the oil in a nonstick frying pan over medium heat. Carefully put the lentil patties into the pan.

7 Cook the patties on one side for 10 minutes, then turn them over using a spatula and cook them on the other side for another 10 minutes.

Pilau Rice with Fruit and Nuts

This rice dish can be a main course or a side dish. The fruits and nuts are very good at balancing the spiciness of dishes such as spicy okra (see page 26) or shrimp patia (see page 18).

What you need

2 cups water
1 vegetable stock cube
1 onion
1 tbsp oil
1 tsp ground coriander (see page 13)
½ tsp ground cumin
2 tbsp raisins
¼ cup canned pineapple chunks
2 tbsp cashew nuts
1 cup rice

What you do

1 Put the water into a pan and bring it to a **boil**. Crumble the stock cube into the water and stir until it **dissolves**. Put the stock to one side.

2 **Peel** the skin from the onion and finely **chop** half of it.

3 Heat the oil in a saucepan over medium heat. Add the chopped onion, coriander, and cumin, and **fry** for five minutes.

4 Add the raisins and pineapple and fry for another five minutes.

5 Add the cashew nuts, vegetable stock, and rice, and bring the mixture to a boil.

6 Reduce the heat to low. **Cover** the pan and **simmer**, stirring occasionally to stop the rice from sticking to the pan. Cook for about 20 minutes or until all the liquid has been soaked up and the rice is soft.

CASHEW NUTS

Cashew trees are common in India. Their nuts are used in lots of Indian dishes. They can be added whole, as in this dish, or ground up to make a type of flour, which is used to thicken sauces.

Chapatis

Chapatis are soft, flat circles of bread. They are eaten with many different Indian dishes and are often used as a scoop to pick up food.

What you need

1¼ cups all-purpose flour
½ tsp salt
½ cup water

What you do

1 Put the salt and 1 cup (125 g) of the flour into a bowl.

2 Gradually stir in the water. Mix well until the mixture forms a **dough**.

3 **Sprinkle** the rest of the flour onto a worktop. Turn the dough out of the bowl and **knead** it for about 10 minutes, until it is smooth.

4 Divide the dough into six pieces. Using a rolling pin, roll out each piece of dough into a thin circle.

5 Heat a nonstick frying pan over medium heat, without adding any oil. Put one chapati into the pan.

6 Cook the chapati for about one minute, until it has brown patches. Turn it over using a spatula and cook the other side for another minute.

7 Cook the rest of the chapatis in the same way.

INDIAN BREADS

Bread is very popular in India. It can be **baked**, fried, or **broiled**. In many cities you can find bread sellers called "tandoor wallahs." They set up portable ovens called tandoors on street corners and use them to cook bread for the nearby households.

Sweet Corn and Coconut Salad

This salad is an ideal accompaniment to a spicy main course. It is quick and easy to make, too.

What you need

- ½ cup frozen sweet corn
- 1 tbsp fresh cilantro leaves (see page 13)
- ½ cup dried coconut
- 2 tbsp lemon juice
- ¼ tsp chili powder (optional)

What you do

 1 Put the sweet corn into a saucepan. Add enough water to cover it.

2 Bring to a **boil**, then reduce the heat. **Simmer** the sweet corn for five minutes.

3 **Drain** the water from the sweet corn by emptying the pan into a sieve or **colander**.

4 Run cold water over the sweet corn to cool it, then put it into a salad bowl.

5 **Chop** the cilantro leaves, then add them to the salad bowl.

6 Add the dried coconut, lemon juice, and chili powder (if using) to the salad bowl.

7 Mix everything together well, then serve.

SWEET CORN

Sweet corn is grown all over India. The grains of the corn are often used as a vegetable, as in this dish. They can also be ground into a type of flour, which is used to make bread and thicken sauces.

Raita

Because many Indian dishes are quite spicy, they are often accompanied by light, fresh dishes such as raita. The main ingredient in raita is yogurt, which can be mixed with other ingredients, such as vegetables and herbs.

what you need

½ cup plain yogurt
1 tbsp fresh cilantro leaves (see page 13)
¼ tsp nutmeg

what you do

1 Put the yogurt into a small bowl.

2 Finely **chop** the cilantro and add it to the yogurt.

3 Add the nutmeg.

4 Mix everything together, then serve.

raisin raita

mixed raita

plain raita

mint raita

potato raita

MORE RAITA RECIPES
There are many different variations to the basic raita.
You may like to try some of them.

MIXED RAITA
Chop a 1-in. (3-cm) long piece of cucumber, 1 onion,
and 1 tomato into small pieces. Add them to the
basic raita.

RAISIN RAITA
Add 1 tbsp raisins to the basic raita.

MINT RAITA
Finely chop 1 tbsp fresh mint leaves.
Add them to the basic raita.

POTATO RAITA
Wash a medium potato, then chop it into small pieces.
Boil the potato pieces in enough water to cover them
for five minutes. **Drain** the potatoes, then add them to
the basic raita.

Banana Fritters

The bananas and sugar in this dish make an ideal change of taste from the spicy, savory Indian main courses.

What you need

2 eggs
1 tbsp sugar
2 tbsp all-purpose flour
½ cup milk
3 bananas
1 tbsp oil

What you do

1. Crack the eggs into a large bowl. **Beat** them with a fork or a whisk until the yolk and the white are mixed.

2. Add the sugar, flour, and milk. Mix everything together well.

3. **Peel** the bananas and **slice** them. Add them to the bowl.

4. Heat the oil in a frying pan over medium heat. Carefully spoon all the banana fritter mixture into the frying pan.

5. Gently **fry** the fritter for five minutes, then turn it over with a spatula and cook the other side for another five minutes.

6. Slide the fritter onto a plate and cut it into four portions.

EXPENSIVE DECORATION

Indian desserts are sometimes decorated with tissue-thin sheets of real silver called "varaq." The silver may be wrapped around nuts that are then placed on top of the food, or simply draped over the dish. On very special occasions, pure gold may be used instead!

Indian Fruit Salad

Tropical fruits and spices give this fruit salad its typically Indian flavor.

What you need

1 pear
1 apple
1 mango
¼ cup fresh or 2 cups
   canned pineapple
1 large banana
2 tbsp sugar
½ tsp ground cumin
Juice of 1 lime

What you do

1 **Chop** all the fruit into bite-sized pieces and place in a large bowl.

2 Mix the sugar, cumin, and lime juice together in a bowl.

3 **Sprinkle** the mixture onto the fruit.

4 Allow to the fruit to **chill** in the refrigerator for an hour before serving.

5 Serve with plain yogurt.

Lassi

Lassi is a traditional Indian drink, which is served as an accompaniment to a meal. Lassi comes in both savory and sweet versions. The savory version is called *lassi namkeen*, and the sweet version is called *lassi meethi*.

What you need

Savory lassi:
6 ice cubes
¾ cup plain yogurt
½ cup milk
¼ tsp ground cumin

Sweet lassi:
6 ice cubes
1 mango
¾ cup plain yogurt
½ cup milk
2 tsp sugar

What you do
Savory Lassi

1 Wrap the ice cubes in a dish towel and crush them with a rolling pin.

2 Put all the other ingredients into a blender or food processor.

3 **Blend** everything together on the highest setting.

4 Put the crushed ice into two glasses.

5 Pour the lassi over the ice, into the glasses.

Sweet Lassi

1 Wrap the ice cubes in a dish towel and crush them with a rolling pin.

2 **Peel** the mango and remove the pit from the middle.

3 Cut the mango into pieces.

4 Put the mango pieces, yogurt, milk, and sugar into a blender or food processor.

5 Blend everything together on the highest setting.

6 Put the crushed ice into two glasses.

7 Pour the lassi over the ice, into the glasses.

VARIATIONS

Another popular drink in India is buttermilk. Buttermilk is the milky liquid that is left when cream is made into butter. In India, buttermilk is often drunk with breakfast or lunch. When you find it in a store, try it and see what you think.

Further Information

Here are some places to find out more about life in India and Indian cooking.

Books

Goodman, Polly. *Food in India* (*Food Around the World*). New York: PowerKids, 2008.

Locricchio, Matthew. *The Second International Cookbook for Kids*. Tarrytown, N.Y.: Marshall Cavendish, 2008.

Madavan, Vijay. *Cooking the Indian Way* (*Easy Menu Ethnic Cookbooks*). Minneapolis: Lerner, 2008.

Sheen, Barbara. *Foods of India* (*A Taste of Culture*). Detroit: KidHaven, 2006.

Websites

http://indianfood.about.com/od/thebasics/a/nevercooked.htm

http://indian-food.suite101.com/article.cfm/a_history_of_indian_food

www.historyforkids.org/learn/india/food

www.globalgourmet.com/destinations/india/

Healthy Eating

This diagram shows the types and proportion of food you should eat to stay healthy. Eat plenty of foods from the *grains* group and plenty from the *fruits* and *vegetables* groups. Eat some foods from the *milk* group and the *meat and beans* group. Foods from the *oils* group are not necessary for a healthy diet, so eat these in small amounts or only occasionally.

Healthy eating, Indian style

In India, most meals include rice, chapatis, or naan bread, which all take up a large section of this plate. Some people eat some chicken and fish, but many people are **vegetarian** and eat beans and lentils instead. You can see how healthy Indian cooking is, with its spicy vegetable dishes and cooling salads!

↑ The MyPyramid food pyramid shows the proportion of food from each food group you should eat to achieve a healthy, balanced diet. This takes into account everything you eat, including snacks.

Glossary

bake cook something in the oven

beat mix something together strongly using a fork, spoon, or whisk

blend mix ingredients together in a blender or food processor

boil cook a liquid on the stove top. Boiling liquid bubbles and steams strongly.

broil cook by being exposed to direct heat

caste grouping of people from highest to lowest

chill put something in the refrigerator to make it cold before serving it

chop cut something into pieces using a knife

colander bowl-shaped container with holes in it, used for draining vegetables and straining

cover put a lid on a pan, or foil over a dish

dissolve mix something until it disappears into a liquid

dough soft mixture of flour and liquid that sticks together and can be shaped or rolled out

drain remove liquid, usually by pouring something into a colander or sieve

fertile land that is capable of growing crops

fry cook something in oil in a pan

grate break something, such as cheese, into small pieces using a grater

grind crush something, such as the seed of a spice plant, until it is a powder

knead keep pressing and pushing dough with your hands so that it becomes very soft and stretchy

monsoon seasonal storms that bring heavy winds

peel remove the skin of a fruit or vegetable

protein body-building material found in some foods such as beans, eggs, and meat

sacred holy, or respected because of religious laws

simmer cook a liquid on the stove top. Simmering liquid bubbles and steams gently.

slice cut something into thin, flat pieces

sprinkle scatter small pieces or drops onto something

thaw defrost something that has been frozen

toast heat in a pan without any oil

tropical hot, wet climate

vegetarian food that does not contain meat or fish. People who don't eat meat or fish are called vegetarians.

Index